The Spirit

Tim Mayfield

with illustrations by Taffy
Series Editor: James Jones

Part One: The Story of the Spirit
1. The Spirit of Jesus
2. That's my boy!
3. Into the desert
4. Power to serve
5. Wait for the gift
6. Wind and flame
7. The Spirit is for everyone!
8. The bridge-builder

Part Two: Pictures of the Spirit
9. Living water
10. The fruit of the Spirit
11. The helper
12. The referee
13. The guide
14. God's mirror
15. Jug of love
16. Adopted by God
17. God's tool-box
18. Mine one day
19. Clean inside
20. The lodger
21. Thick skin
22. Come!
23. In his footsteps

Part Three: The Spirit and You
24. Born of the Spirit
25. The father's joy
26. Drenched with God
27. Receive the gift
28. Keep re-fuelling
29. Hurting love
30. Porta-temples
31. My witnesses

The Bible Reading Fellowship

1

Lee was heartbroken. His new CD player had been stolen. But later that day a police car drew up outside. The officer marched up the drive . . . with Lee's missing system.

'Wow!' said Lee, overjoyed. 'How did you get it back so quickly?' 'Simple,' said the officer. He took an ultraviolet torch from his pocket and shone it on the CD player. On the side was Lee's postcode. Unknown to him his Dad had written it there with a special pen. Then no-one could see it till they used the right kind of light.

As with that unseen message, so with God. No one had ever seen him. But when the time was right, the Holy Spirit made him visible. That time was the first Christmas, when Jesus was born . . .

The Spirit of Jesus

1

Read Matthew 1:18–20

This was how the birth of Jesus Christ took place. His mother Mary was engaged to Joseph, but before they were married, she found out that she was going to have a baby by the Holy Spirit. Joseph was a man who always did right, but he did not want to disgrace Mary publicly; so he made plans to break the engagement privately. While he was thinking about this, an angel of the Lord appeared to him in a dream and said, 'Joseph, descendant of David, do not be afraid to take Mary to be your wife. For it is by the Holy Spirit that she has conceived. She will have a son, and you will name him Jesus— because he will save his people from their sins.'

The birth of Jesus was the work of the Holy Spirit. He came to show us what God had always been like. So if you want to know God . . . look at Jesus.

Jesus came to show us what God is like. So look at this list of things Jesus did. Each of them shows us something about God. Number them 1–6 in order of importance for you . . .

____ He spoke up for the poor

____ He told people good news

____ He was interested in ordinary people

____ He healed the sick

____ He taught people how to pray

____ He showed people how much God loved them

Holy Spirit, through Mary you brought Jesus into the world, showing us God. Thank you. Amen.

2

That's my boy!

Read Matthew 3:16–17

As soon as Jesus was baptised, he came up out of the water. Then heaven was opened to him, and he saw the Spirit of God coming down on him like a dove and alighting on him. Then a voice said from heaven, 'This is my own dear Son, with whom I am pleased.'

It was the local under-17's rugby cup final. In the dressing room Nick's heart was pounding. Last few words from the captain, and they ran out.

Over two hundred people were there. But Nick couldn't miss that voice: 'Come on blue!' It was his Dad. He'd made it after all. They caught each other's eye. Dad winked. Nick felt two inches taller.

After he was born, Jesus spent thirty years learning carpentry. Then he began his public work for God. As he stepped out, his Father was there, cheering him on . . .

The Spirit brought Jesus to birth. Now, at the beginning of his new work for God, the Spirit is there again. This time he's come to show Jesus he's not alone. The Father is with him and loves him.

As with Jesus, so with us. The Holy Spirit works in us to bring God close. He tells us how much the Father loves us. He shows us we're not alone, because God is cheering us on.

Shade in the bar to the extent that each statement is true for you . . .

2

God feels very close to me

Not true				True

When I face difficulties
I know I'm not alone

Not true				True

I really believe that God loves me

Not true				True

Thank you Holy Spirit. At the beginning of Jesus' work you showed him he was not alone. Work in me, too. Bring God close, show me the Father's love, and tell me I'm never alone. Amen.

THAT'S MY BOY!!

3

Imagine you're the pilot of a single seater aircraft. You crash in the desert. You have enough water, but no food. It's over a month before you're rescued. What's the worst thing about your ordeal? (Tick one)

☐ Terrible hunger pains
☐ Freezing cold nights
☐ The blazing midday heat
☐ Feeling completely alone
☐ Worrying about what's going to happen
☐ Being tempted to give in
☐ Other ....

We've seen that when Jesus was baptized, the Holy Spirit made God feel very close. But the Spirit doesn't only do nice things to us. Look what he did to Jesus as soon as he was baptized . . .

Read Luke 4:1–2a

> Jesus returned from the Jordan full of the Holy Spirit and was led by the Spirit into the desert, where he was tempted by the Devil for forty days.

Jesus had a wonderful experience when he was baptized. But straightaway he was taken into the desert. You've already seen how difficult life is in the desert. But Jesus was there for forty days.

It's just the same for us. Sometimes the Holy Spirit will make us happier than we dared to hope. But not always. At other times the Spirit will take us into very difficult places.

God will still be with us. And, in time, the Holy Spirit will lead us on into easier places. Then we'll find out that what the Spirit did was good for us. Our faith

Into the desert

is stronger. We know God better. We know *the power of the Spirit*.

What's the most difficult time you've had as a Christian?

....
....
....

What did you learn about God from that experience?

....
....
....

Holy Spirit, you led Jesus into the desert. Now take me wherever you want. I'll go where you lead me. Just show me more of God and never let me go. Amen.

I'VE JUST GOT TO KNOW!! HOW'S WEST HAM BEEN DOING!?

RESCUE

4

It came from nowhere. I was driving down the motorway when suddenly this enormous lorry filled the rear-view mirror. It came bearing down upon us and flashed all its headlights.

I pulled into the inside lane and it carved past us. I had to laugh: written across the back it said 'the power to serve'.

There are two kinds of power. There's the power of the juggernaut, pushing people onto the hard shoulder. And there's the power of Jesus, which works to help people and set them free.

Luke tells us that after his time in the desert, Jesus *returned to Galilee, and the power of the Holy Spirit was with him.*

Power was with him. But it wasn't a power for himself. He used his power for others. For him, it was truly the power to serve...

Read Luke 4:18–19

The Spirit of the Lord is upon me, because he has chosen me to bring good news to the poor. He has sent me to proclaim liberty to the captives and recovery of sight to the blind; to set free the oppressed and announce that the time has come when the Lord will save his people.

Jesus promised that one day his Holy Spirit would give his power to his followers. That promise is for you, today. But the power of Jesus is never for kicks. His power is there to help you help other people. It is the power to serve.

Who do you know whom you could serve? Tick the ones that might apply to you...

☐ The teenagers on your estate who don't know God
☐ A member of your family who is poorly
☐ A lonely person who lives on their own
☐ Poor people overseas who haven't enough food
☐ Someone who is shy, and new to your school
☐ A single parent with several pre-school children

Now choose one of the people you've ticked. Write one thing you might do to serve them...

....

....

Power to serve

4

Holy Spirit, I don't want to live for myself. I want to help other people. So fill me with the Spirit of Jesus. Give me the power to serve. Amen.

5

Wait for

Here's a list of things people wait for. Tick the things that will happen if people wait long enough...

- ☐ Your favourite team winning the cup
- ☐ Your train arriving at the station
- ☐ A white Christmas
- ☐ Your birthday
- ☐ The end of the school term
- ☐ Manned space flight to Mars
- ☐ The discovery of the Loch Ness Monster
- ☐ The next Olympics

All his life, Albert had done the pools. Every Saturday he waited by the radio. Every Saturday he marked his coupon. He dreamed of winning a million. It never happened. Albert died last week.

Sarfraz couldn't wait to be seventeen. His Dad had promised him driving lessons as soon as he was old enough. One morning Sarfraz jumped out of bed. The day had come! It was his birthday. He was seventeen.

Some people, like Albert, wait and wait for something which might never happen. Others, like Sarfraz, wait for things which will, in time, take place.

There is a world of difference between the two kinds of waiting...

5

the gift

Read Luke 24:49

> And I myself will send upon you what my Father has promised. But you must wait in the city until the power from above comes down upon you.

Jesus told his disciples to wait. But they were waiting for something God had promised. So they knew, like Sarfraz, that if they waited long enough, it would happen.

It's just the same for us. God wants us to be more open to his Spirit. So we are to wait patiently, like the disciples. Then, at the right moment, which God will choose, his Spirit will give us more power.

Take some time to be quiet. Clench your fists. Open them slowly. As you do, open yourself to God and be ready for whatever he wants to give you.

6 Wind an

God had promised it. Jesus told his followers to wait for it. So because they waited, and because God had promised it, 'it' happened . . .

Read Acts 2:1–4

> When the day of Pentecost came, all the believers were gathered together in one place. Suddenly there was a noise from the sky which sounded like a strong wind blowing, and it filled the whole house where they were sitting. Then they saw what looked like tongues of fire which spread out and touched each person there. They were all filled with the Holy Spirit and began to talk in other languages, as the Spirit enabled them to speak.

For centuries God's people had been looking forward to this moment. Now it was happening. God was pouring out his Holy Spirit upon ordinary people.

God wanted those first disciples to understand what was happening to them. So he spoke to them in pictures: the strong wind and the tongues of fire.

The strong wind is a picture of God's power. Try and pitch a tent in a force nine gale. You'll know that wind is power.

The tongues of fire are a picture of being all out for God. You might have heard people say 'I'm all fired up'.

That's just what happened on the first day of Pentecost. God's power filled those early disciples, and they caught fire for Jesus.

d flame

6

Think first about the wind, the power of God. What part of your life most needs God's power? Write it here.

....

....

Now think about the flame. Read the sentence below and then honestly mark on the 0–10 scale how much it applies to you...

    I want to be on fire for God.

0 1 2 3 4 5 6 7 8 9 10

Lord Jesus, you gave your people power, and set them on fire for you. Do the same for me today. Amen.

> I DON'T CARE IF THIS WIND DOES MAKE YOU THINK OF GOD!! HELP ME PUT THIS TENT UP WILL YOU?!!

7

In the first column rank each person in order of their importance to you.

Doctor		
Soldier		
Criminal		
Policeman		
Tramp		
Waitress		
Teacher		
Bank Manager		
Nurse		
Engineer		

Now in the second column, rank each person as you feel they would be important to God.

It's a trick question, isn't it? For we know that all people matter to God. No matter what they do. No matter what they've done. All people matter to God.

People haven't always seen it that way, though. Before Jesus came, the Holy Spirit was only for special people (kings, prophets) to help them do special jobs.

But on the day of Pentecost, when God poured out the Holy Spirit on all Jesus' followers, Peter remembered a promise from the Old Testament. He told the gathering crowd all about it.

Read Acts 2:15–18

> *These people are not drunk, as you suppose; it is only nine o'clock in the morning. Instead, this is what the*

The Spirit is

7

prophet Joel spoke about: 'This is what I will do in the last days, God says: I will pour out my Spirit on everyone. Your sons and daughters will proclaim my message; your young men will see visions, and your old men will have dreams. Yes, even on my servants, both men and women, I will pour out my Spirit in those days, and they will proclaim my message.'

Once, the Spirit had been for special people. But the prophet Joel dreamed of a time when the Holy Spirit would be for all people. 'That time is now,' said Peter.

We're living in the time after Pentecost. God hasn't changed. Whoever you are. Wherever you come from. Whatever you've done. However long you've been a Christian... the Spirit is for you. Believe it, and receive him.

Father God, you want to pour out your Spirit on everyone so that we can proclaim your message. Help me to believe I matter to you and fill me with your Spirit. Amen.

for everyone!

8
The bridge-builder

Read Acts 10:44–48

While Peter was still speaking, the Holy Spirit came down on all those who were listening to his message. The Jewish believers who had come from Joppa with Peter were amazed that God had poured out his gift of the Holy Spirit on the Gentiles also. For they heard them speaking in strange tongues and praising God's greatness. Peter spoke up: 'These people have received the Holy Spirit, just as we also did. Can anyone, then,

People hate each other for all kinds of reasons. Some people hate other people if their skin is a different colour. Some people hate other people if they vote for a different political party. Some people even hate people if they support a different football team.

In the time of Jesus, many Jews hated people who were not Jews. They called them 'Gentiles'. So there were only two kinds of people. You were either a 'Jew', or you were a 'Gentile'.

This gave Jesus' first followers a problem. Could non-Jews (common 'Gentiles') join the church, or not? Was the church to be just for Jews? Or could non-Jews join in? The argument rumbled for some time ... until the Holy Spirit settled it ...

stop them from being baptised with water?' So he ordered them to be baptised in the name of Jesus Christ.

The Holy Spirit is God's great bridge-builder. He's been doing it for thousands of years. It all began on that day when both Jews and non-Jews were filled with the Spirit.

It's still happening today. Where Christians from whatever branch of the church discover the Holy Spirit, they discover that petty differences no longer matter. They find that what ever 'denomination' they belong to isn't the point. The point is that they know God's Spirit to be at work in their lives. For the Spirit loves to build bridges. He loves to bring people together.

Look at the picture of the bridge. Either side, write the names of people or groups who don't get on (e.g. 'Protestants' and 'Catholics', or the names of some friends who have fallen out). Then pray for the Holy Spirit to bring them together, like he did with the Jews and the Gentiles.

Father, you hurt when people hate each other. Please send your Holy Spirit between the people I've named. Build a bridge between them, and help them to get on. Amen.

9

What a moment. The promising teenager sprinter has won Olympic gold. She stands, medal round her neck, on top of the podium. Her national anthem plays, her country's flag eases up the pole. She has a huge lump in her throat and tears roll down her cheeks. The commentator is beside himself. 'Look at her drinking in this moment... soaking up the atmosphere...'

There's nothing there to drink of course. But the commentator tells us she's drinking in the atmosphere. He means she's making the most of her moment. She's really alive to what's going on. She wants to soak up every scrap of her achievement.

If that makes sense, you'll understand what Jesus means when he invites you to 'come to me and drink'. He wants you to drink in his presence. To be really alive to God as you worship him.

Jesus said:

> Whoever is thirsty should come to me, and whoever believes in me should drink. As the scripture says, 'Streams of life-giving water will pour out from his side.' Jesus said this about the Spirit, which those who believed in him were going to receive. At that time the Spirit had not yet been given, because Jesus had not been raised to glory.
>
> John 7:37–39

Let's actually see what Jesus means. Take a rectangular pie dish and fill it with water to about an inch deep. Then take several sheets of kitchen roll folded together. The kitchen roll is you, when you haven't really worshipped God for a while: all dry and in need of a drink.

Now place the kitchen roll in the water. Watch it soak up the water. Picture yourself drinking in the presence of God, soaking up the reality of his love. Then decide, next time you're in prayer or worship, to come to Jesus and drink: to make the most of the moment, like the sprinter with Olympic gold.

Lord Jesus, forgive me when my mind's not on the job. When I don't really pray, when I don't really worship, I get all dry inside. Next time I'll make the most of the moment. I'll drink in your presence. Amen.

Living water

10

The fruit of the Spirit

We drove for fifteen miles through the desert. The landscape was bare. Hardly anything grew.

Then we drove into Jericho. Everything changed. Jericho is built by one of the biggest fresh water springs in the Middle East. Everywhere there were fruit trees. They groaned under the weight of oranges, limes, lemons. I bought a grapefruit the size of a football.

Jericho is a real life oasis. It shows that the desert isn't dead. It's teeming with life. It just needs water to wake it up.

St Paul understood the link between water and fruit. He knew that where people spend long enough drinking God's living water, their lives produce all kinds of lovely qualities. He called them 'the fruit of the Spirit'.

Read Galatians 5:22–23

> But the Spirit produces love, joy, peace, patience, kindness, goodness, faithfulness, humility, and self-control. There is no law against such things as these.

Just as all kinds of fruits grow where there's water, so our lives change when we drink in the Holy Spirit. But how 'fruitful' are we? This exercise will help us find out.

Each of the statements below is based on one part of the fruit of the Spirit. On the 0–10 scale mark how true each of them is for you.

All I do springs from love for God and for other people.
0 1 2 3 4 5 6 7 8 9 10

Underlying all my moods there is a deep joy.
0 1 2 3 4 5 6 7 8 9 10

10

I'm often under pressure, but through it all I'm at peace.
0 1 2 3 4 5 6 7 8 9 10

I'm a patient person, both with difficult people and with difficult jobs.
0 1 2 3 4 5 6 7 8 9 10

When people look at me they see a kind person.
0 1 2 3 4 5 6 7 8 9 10

I'm willing to see good in other people, and not to run them down.
0 1 2 3 4 5 6 7 8 9 10

I stick by my friends and family, through good times and through bad.
0 1 2 3 4 5 6 7 8 9 10

I never push myself to the front, but am happy to see the spotlight fall on others.
0 1 2 3 4 5 6 7 8 9 10

When I'm tempted to get very angry, I can control that instinct and not take it out on those around me.
0 1 2 3 4 5 6 7 8 9 10

If you're happy with your score... great! You must be a good person to know. If you're not... don't despair. Make time to drink in God's Holy Spirit. Let him grow an oasis of fruit in you.

Father, when we drink from your Spirit our lives change. Help me today to come to the living water: then grow your fruit in me. Amen.

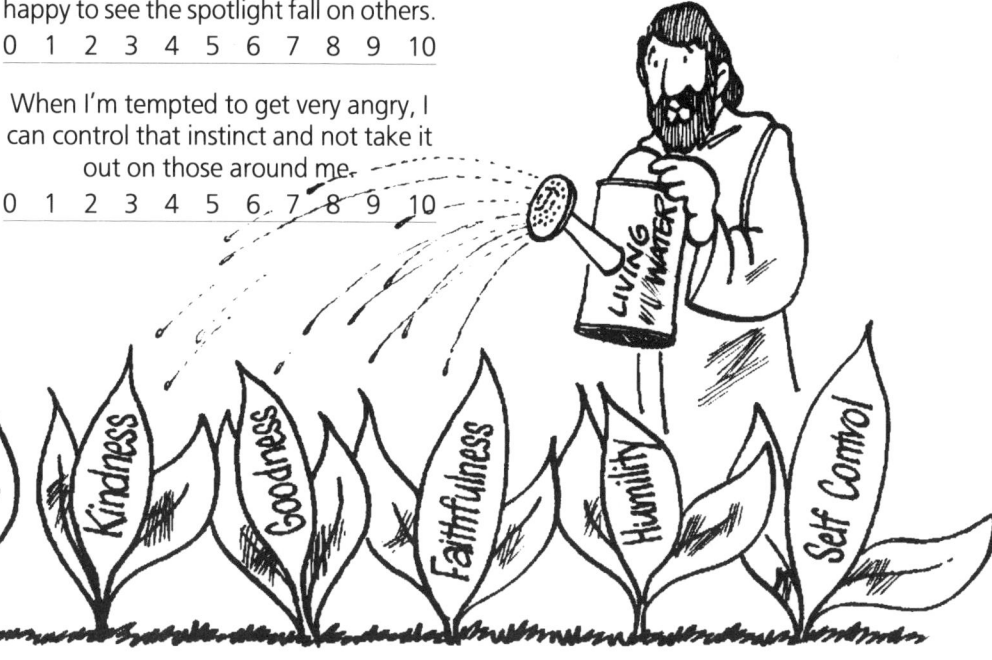

11

Gavin had always hated cross country. All those hills.. the mud.. your legs about to drop off.

But that day was different. The Olympic champion had come to Gavin's school. And here he was, running alongside him.

'That's it: regular breathing. Keep your arms pumping. You're doing brilliantly. Nearly there now. Drive to the top of this next hill, then it's downhill all the way. Fantastic.'

Gavin flew round the course that day. A genius was alongside him. He taught him how to run better. And the champion's confidence and strength seemed to flow into him.

Sometimes being a Christian can be hard work. Like slogging round a muddy cross country course. But never attempt it in your own strength! Jesus, by his Spirit, wants to run alongside you.

Read John 14:15–17

> If you love me, you will obey my commandments. I will ask the Father, and he will give you another Helper, who will stay with you for ever. He is the Spirit who reveals the truth about God. The world cannot receive him, because it cannot see him or know him. But you know him, because he remains with you and is in you.

THE HELPER

11

By his Spirit Jesus won't just be alongside you. He'll be inside you. He'll give you the strength to go on. He'll teach you how to live. He'll encourage you all the way to the finish.

Tick the ways in which the Holy Spirit has encouraged you to keep on.

- ☐ Inspiring worship
- ☐ Encouragement from a friend
- ☐ Answered prayer
- ☐ A special event that meant a lot to you
- ☐ Showing you a special message from the Bible
- ☐ Other ....

....

Jesus, you know it's hard sometimes. When I'm struggling, send me your Helper Spirit, and encourage me to the finish. Amen.

THAT'S GREAT! KEEP IT UP!!

12

Dave gasped in horror. Two minutes left as the ball flew past the keeper. The net bulged. The opposing fans exploded into a riot of colour. Surely the cup had been lost.

Then it was Dave's turn to cheer. The referee blew his whistle. But not to signal a goal. The 'scorer' had been offside. The goal didn't count. It was still 1–1 and extra time loomed.

It's the referee's job to control the game. All the while the players keep to the rules, he allows play to continue. As soon as someone strays offside, he blows the whistle. It wouldn't be fair otherwise. It'd be chaos.

For those who allow him to, the Holy Spirit acts just like a referee.

Read Romans 8:5

Those who live as their human nature tells them to, have their minds controlled by what human nature wants. Those who live as the Spirit tells them to, have their minds controlled by what the Spirit wants.

We've got a choice, you and I. We can shut the Spirit out of our lives, and control them ourselves. Or we can ask him to come and control them for us, and blow the whistle when we're offside.

I thank God for the times the Spirit's done that for me. When I let God down by something I do or say, I'm glad he tells me. He does it because he wants the best for me. He wants me to stay close to God and let him control my life.

The referee

12

FOUL!!

The Spirit's whistle is our conscience. That's the part of our mind that tells us we're offside. Look at the list below. Tick the ones that would make the referee Spirit blow his whistle.

- ☐ Stealing
- ☐ Giving
- ☐ Thanking
- ☐ Bullying
- ☐ Forgiving
- ☐ Lying
- ☐ Sharing
- ☐ Helping
- ☐ Teasing
- ☐ Cheating

Holy Spirit, I want you to control my life. Come into my mind, sharpen my conscience, blow the whistle when I'm offside, and show me how to live. Amen.

13
The guide

We leant on the dry stone wall by the stile and drank in the view. Fantastic scenery lay spread out below us. But where next? The path branched into two. We reached for the guidebook. 'At a stile over a dry stone wall take the right fork towards a farmhouse with an ornate chimney.'

Someone spotted the chimney in the distance. We knew we were on the right track.

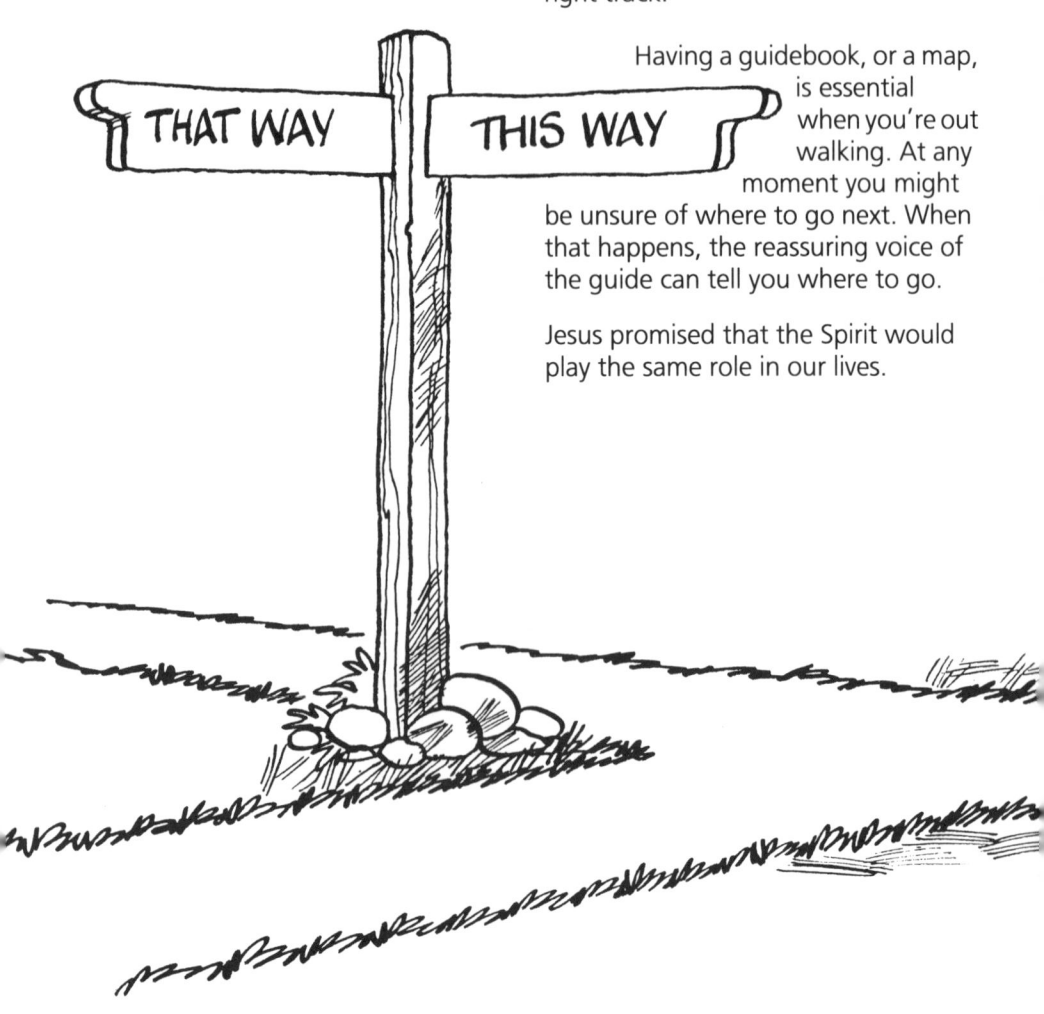

Having a guidebook, or a map, is essential when you're out walking. At any moment you might be unsure of where to go next. When that happens, the reassuring voice of the guide can tell you where to go.

Jesus promised that the Spirit would play the same role in our lives.

13

Read John 16:12–13a

> I have much more to tell you, but now it would be too much for you to bear. When, however, the Spirit comes, who reveals the truth about God, he will lead you into all the truth.

At many points in our life we can be unsure of where to go next. Unsure of what to believe about God. Unsure as to what he's like. Unsure about a big decision we have to take.

But next time you're unsure, remember Jesus' promise. *The Spirit . . . will lead you into all the truth.* The truth about where next. The truth about you. The truth about God.

If the Holy Spirit guides us . . . how does he do it?

Look at the list. Put in order from 1 to 10 the ways he's guided you:

____ Through a strong feeling inside
____ Through other people
____ Through worship
____ Through sermons
____ Through prayers
____ Through speaking into my mind
____ Through 'coincidence'
____ Through my conscience
____ Through receiving Holy Communion
____ Through the Bible

Jesus, thank you for your promise. Your Spirit will guide me into all the truth. Teach me to listen for his guidance and to follow where he leads. Amen.

P.S. If you think God is guiding you, don't forget to test that calling: talk it through with an older Christian.

14 God's

During a geography class at school there was a partial eclipse of the sun. This was very good timing for the teacher, who used it to fill a good fifteen minutes of the lesson.

The only thing was... if you looked at the sun you were soon dazzled. You couldn't see what was happening. Then some bright spark hit on a good idea. By positioning the classroom windows properly you could look at the sun's reflection in the window, and see the edge of the moon creep across the edge of the sun.

Hold that picture in your mind as you read through Jesus' words about the Holy Spirit.

> He will give me glory, because he will take what I say and tell it to you. All that my Father has is mine; that is why I said that the Spirit will take what I give him and tell it to you.
>
> John 16:14–15

How can we possibly hear God? After all, he is the all-powerful creator of the universe: we are so small alongside him. He is totally pure: we are so dirty and selfish alongside him. Like the sun we thought about earlier, he is a dazzling light. How dare we say we know what he's like?

We dare because of the work of the Holy Spirit. Our classroom window reflected the brightness and helped us to look at the sun. In just the same way the Holy Spirit helps us to see the Father. The Spirit takes what belongs to the Father and makes it known to us. He is God's mirror: reflecting to us God's glory in ways we can understand.

mirror mirror

14

Which of these things about God has the Holy Spirit shown you?

- ☐ He is passionately concerned for the poor
- ☐ He always forgives us when we ask him from the heart
- ☐ He is terribly angered by the injustice of the world
- ☐ He hurts with people who hurt
- ☐ He wants all people to get to know him better

Holy Spirit, without you I could not see God. Thank you for taking what belongs to the Father, and telling it to me. Amen.

15

Nearly every time archaeologists find an ancient village, they find containers. Things to put water in: cups, jugs, pitchers, jars and bowls.

Ever wondered why that is? Isn't it because we need water so much? And as soon as we need water, we need something to put it in, before it dribbles off into the ground.

We have other needs too. Water, food, oxygen... they're all for our bodies. But your body isn't your real 'you'. Your real 'you' needs things like friends, hope, understanding... and love. That's why you'll find a whacking great jug of love at the heart of God.

Read Romans 5:5

> ...God has poured out his love into our hearts by means of the Holy Spirit, who is God's gift to us.

See? The Holy Spirit is God's jug. He is filled to overflowing with the love of God. Whenever anyone opens himself to God, that love is poured in.

What's stopping you from receiving that love? It could be that you can't quite bring yourself to believe that God loves you that much. It could be that you've seen awful things, which make you doubt that God is there. It could be that you don't know what 'love' means, because of things that other people did to you (or didn't do for you).

Whatever it is that's holding you back... God loves you. So make time to be still. Ask God to pour his love into you. Picture yourself as a vase, being filled up with pure, cool water: the water of life.

Look at the heart shape. Colour it in to the extent that you feel you've received the love of God.

Father, you know I find it hard sometimes. Often there isn't enough love around so I doubt that you can love me. But come, Holy Spirit. Pour your love into me: show me what 'love' means. Amen.

Jug of love

15

16
Adopted by God

In that moment, Mark's life was shattered. His parents, driving back from a night out, had skidded out of control. Both died instantly. Mark, an only child, was left on his own.

For a while, Mark lived with relations here and there. But he felt lost and alone. Then one day he heard that his Uncle Graham and Auntie Sue wanted to adopt him.

The news made Mark feel happier than he'd felt for months. He'd only met Graham and Sue two or three times. But he'd always like them, and enjoyed playing with their children.

The adoption went through, and Mark was made to feel really at home. He now has two adopted brothers and a sister. They all get on really well.

What Graham and Sue did for Mark is a picture of what the Holy Spirit does for us. Before we knew God it's like we were orphans. Saint Paul writes that God's Spirit changes all that.

Read Romans 8:15–17a

For the Spirit that God has given you does not make you slaves and cause you to be afraid; instead, the Spirit makes you God's children, and by the Spirit's power we cry out to God, 'Father! my Father!' God's Spirit joins himself to our spirits to declare that we are God's children. Since we are his children, we will possess the blessings he keeps for his people.

16

Before we knew God we were like orphans. Now that we know God, his Spirit has made us God's children. We share the same Father, and all Christian people are our brothers and sisters.

Look at the family tree below. In the box on the left, write your name. In the remaining four boxes write the names of four other people from your church or youth group.

Dear Father, by your Spirit you adopt me as your child. Thank you that I need never be alone. Thank you for all my brothers and sisters in the church. Amen.

17

It was the TV chef's nightmare. Live on camera demonstrating a ham omelette... and no knife or fork on the workbench. He laughed nervously, broke the eggs into the bowl and mashed them into pulp with his fingers. Then picking up the ham he tore it into pieces with his bare hands and plopped them into the egg mangle. 'There... ha ha ha... easy when you know how!'

There are tools for nearly every job. Forks and knives for your ham omelette. Spanner and screwdriver for your mountain bike.

It's just the same with God. He calls us to a task (building his kingdom) and gives us the right tools for the job. Saint Paul calls them 'The gifts of the Holy Spirit...'

Read 1 Corinthians 12:4–7

> There are different kinds of spiritual gifts, but the same Spirit gives them. There are different ways of serving, but the same Lord is served. There are different abilities to perform service, but the same God gives ability to all for their particular service. The Spirit's presence is shown in some way in each person for the good of all.

If you mean business with God, and really want to serve him, expect him to give you one or more 'gifts of the Spirit'. They're the tools God gives you to do the job. You'd be lost without them.

The Bible gives at least two lists of 'Gifts of the Spirit' (1 Corinthians 12:1–11 and Romans 12:6–9). Find them in the word square, then tick the gift your church needs most.

God's tool box

17

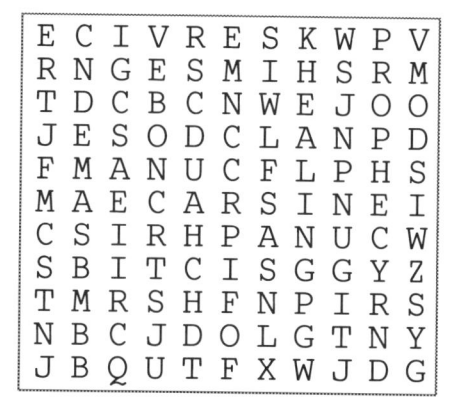

```
E C I V R E S K W P V
R N G E S M I H S R M
T D C B C N W E J O O
J E S O D C L A N P D
F M A N U C F L P H S
M A E C A R S I N E I
C S I R H P A N U C W
S B I T C I S G G Y Z
T M R S H F N P I R S
N B C J D O L G T N Y
J B Q U T F X W J D G
```

☐ Wisdom
☐ Faith
☐ Healing
☐ Miracles
☐ Prophecy (1)
☐ Tongues (2)
☐ Service
☐ Teaching
☐ Encouraging
☐ Kindness

(1) Prophecy: speaking a message from God in your own language.

(2) Tongues: a special prayer language for telling God our deepest feelings.

Holy Spirit, thank you for your gifts. They are the tools we need to do the job. I am open to you. Equip me as you know best. Give me the right gifts at the right time. Amen.

IT'S AS SIMPLE AS THAT!!

18

Mine one day

Look at the list of items. In the first column, estimate how much each would cost. And in the second, put how much you'd want as a deposit if you were the trader.

Fairly good second-hand car		
Antique grandfather clock		
Video recorder		
Computer with five games		
Mountain bike with all the gear		
A human being		

Kicking round town one afternoon, Leroy suddenly saw the sound system of his dreams. He had some money on him, but not enough. He went into the shop and asked if he could leave a deposit. The manager agreed, and slapped a big sticker on the system: 'Sold'.

18

By scraping together all his savings, and by borrowing some off his Mum and Dad, Leroy had the full amount by the following Saturday. The system was still there, because he'd paid his deposit. Now he could take it home. It was his!

Saint Paul uses the picture of the deposit as he explains the Spirit's work in our lives:

> And you also became God's people when you heard the true message, the Good News that brought you salvation. You believed in Christ, and God put his stamp of ownership on you by giving you the Holy Spirit he had promised. The Spirit is the guarantee that we shall receive what God has promised his people.
>
> Ephesians 1:13–14a

The Holy Spirit is God's deposit. He is God's 'stamp of ownership' on us, proving that we are his. He hasn't taken us home yet. But the Spirit is the guarantee that one day God will come and take us home.

Pause for a moment. Imagine God in your church. He is joyfully slapping stickers on people. The stickers say 'MINE'.

Father God, your Spirit in me is a sign that I am yours. Thank you.

19

My Dad has this brilliant way of cleaning out our teapot. Every now and then, when lots of gunk had built up inside, he would de-scale it.

This involved mixing denture powder with hot water in the teapot. The mixture would then fizz and froth for a bit, and when the fizzing had died down . . . presto! All the brown tannin stains had peeled off. The tea pot was as good as new.

In just the same way, the Spirit comes to us to clean us out inside.

Read 1 Peter 1:2

You were chosen according to the purpose of God the Father and were made a holy people by his Spirit, to obey Jesus Christ and be purified by his blood.

Just like our old teapot, all kinds of gunk builds up inside us. We might be jealous of other people. We might have been hurt by someone and refuse to forgive them.

But the Spirit of God is a Holy Spirit.

19

One of the first things he does to us is to clean us up inside. The gunk will still build up again—we're only human. But time and again God's Holy Spirit will come and froth away inside us and make us clean.

What kind of things would the Holy Spirit want to clean out from us? Hidden in the square are at least five items he'd wash out for starters. Using the key letter 'E' in every word, and using the other letters as many times as you like, try and find things the Holy Spirit would want to clean out of us.

Holy Spirit, you know me so well. You know the nasty things that build up inside me. I want you to make me clean. So I open myself to you. Wash me, and make me clean inside. Amen.

E
e.g. 'Envy'

D	B	Y	R
H	A	L	V
W	P	T	G
S	E	N	I

Clean inside

20

The lodger

The Williams family were really up against it. They couldn't get on with each other. Arguments seemed to brew from nothing.

To make matters worse, they ran into money problems. So they decided to take in lodgers, though none of them was looking forward to it.

But after a few weeks of Geoff living with them, they couldn't work out why they'd been so nervous. Geoff was great. Everyone like him. In fact, he was a bit like the missing piece in the jigsaw: the whole family felt better for having him around.

What's more, Geoff was a DIY specialist. He made lots of improvements round the place. Now the Williamses can't imagine life before him.

A lodger, who lives with a family, and makes life better for everyone there. Sounds like another picture of the Holy Spirit.

Read 2 Timothy 1:14

Through the power of the Holy Spirit, who lives in us, keep the good things that have been entrusted to you.

The key words there are *'who lives in us'*. If you're a Christian, then you have a lodger inside: the Holy Spirit of God. So imagine your life is like a house. Score yourself out of ten for each item.

DOORMAT

Are you a welcoming person? Would your doormat say 'Welcome!' Or 'Oh no! Not you again!' Score yourself out of ten for how welcoming you are.

0 1 2 3 4 5 6 7 8 9 10

KITCHEN

Are you happy with what you eat? Or do you binge? Do you eat loads of stuff you know isn't good for you? Score yourself out of ten for how healthily you eat.

0 1 2 3 4 5 6 7 8 9 10

BATHROOM

Are you happy with the way you look? Or do you worry and worry about your appearance? Score yourself out of ten for how happy you feel in your body.

0 1 2 3 4 5 6 7 8 9 10

MONEYBOX

Is your money 'mine all mine'? Or do you have an open moneybox? Score yourself out of ten for how generous you are to your friends and those in need.

0 1 2 3 4 5 6 7 8 9 10

LIVING ROOM

Are you happy with what you watch on TV? Or are there certain programmes you wish you didn't watch? Score yourself out of ten for how healthily you watch.

0 1 2 3 4 5 6 7 8 9 10

Now make a note of one thing the lodger Spirit would want to change inside you.

....

....

Holy Spirit, you live inside me. Like the lodger in the story, please make me a better person. Amen.

21

Why not make a pint of custard? Put 2 tablespoons of custard powder into a large jug, along with 1½ tablespoons of sugar. Then mix that to a paste with a bit of milk taken from 1 pint.

Heat the rest of the milk to nearly boiling, and pour it onto your custard paste, stirring well. Then put the custard back in your saucepan and bring it to the boil, stirring all the time.

Once you have your custard, pour it back into the jug, and leave it for about fifteen minutes. When you come back, you'll find a picture of me when I'm away from God.

When you do come back, you'll find a thick skin on top of the custard. Yuck! You need to peel the skin back before you can pour the custard out.

That's just like what happens to me. When I've been away from God, I go all hard. It's like a thick skin grows over me. I go hard towards other people, and the world doesn't seem as bright as before.

But every time I come back and ask him to, the Holy Spirit makes me new. It's like he peels back the tough layer that's grown inside me. He gives me new life.

Thick skin

ONE LUMP OR TWO?!

21

Read Titus 3:4–5

But when the kindness and love of God our Saviour was revealed, he saved us. It was not because of any good deeds that we ourselves had done, but because of his own mercy that he saved us, through the Holy Spirit, who gives us new birth and new life by washing us.

How thick is your skin? Shade each bar to the extent that each statement is true of you today.

I feel very close to God

Not true   **True**

I'm very aware of the beauty of the world

Not true   **True**

I don't resent other people

Not true   **True**

I'm quick to forgive others

Not true   **True**

The suffering of the world makes a big impression on me

Not true   **True**

Do you feel thick-skinned? Like you want the Holy Spirit to make you new? Pray this prayer.

Holy Spirit, I don't want to be thick skinned. I want to feel close to you. I want to notice the beauty of your world. I want to feel the pain of mankind. So peel back the layers, Holy Spirit, and make me new.
Amen.

22
Come!

Two kinds of people for you to think about. 'Go away!' people and 'Come near!' people:

'Go away!' people love to be on their own. They don't have many friends, would never dream of throwing a party, and could quite possibly have a car sticker that reads 'push off, dog breath'!

'Come near!' people are totally different. They love to be with people. They love to make new friends. And they have an open heart, ready to care for people in need.

Some people think that God is a 'go away!' person. They can't believe he's interested in them. They think they have to be perfect before he'll look their way. They think he wants to squeeze all the fun out of life.

They are wrong. God's Holy Spirit is the biggest 'come near!' person there will ever be.

Read Revelation 22:17

> The Spirit and the Bride say, 'Come!' Everyone who hears this must also say, 'Come!' Come, whoever is thirsty; accept the water of life as a gift, whoever wants it.

Whenever Jesus wanted a picture of heaven, he talked about great parties. The Holy Spirit wants to invite everyone to the party. So he opens his arms wide to us, and says 'come!'

22

Hidden in the word square are 10 words that describe a 'come near!' person. Find them all, then tick the words in the list that describe God himself.

```
G H T F W A R Z S L
Y L E V I L K H U T
L P L S T N S F O D
D H B H D C T M R N
N T A N E H B T E G
E H I P G L F U N H
I K C U P M E I E M
R B O H M Y R L G K
F H S J B A M A I H
T I R A C R N Q W V
```

- ☐ Generous
- ☐ Kind
- ☐ Caring
- ☐ Fun
- ☐ Happy
- ☐ Friendly
- ☐ Warm
- ☐ Thoughtful
- ☐ Sociable
- ☐ Lively

Holy Spirit, you want everyone to 'come near'. I'm sorry for the times I've kept my distance. Now I come to you. Help me to invite others to your party. And at my death, receive me into the great banquet of heaven. Amen.

23 In his footsteps

His head hung limp and their eyes filled with tears. They knew that Jesus was dead. He had promised them so much. Now all they could do was to bury him and go back to their fishing-nets.

But three days later something happened. Those early followers of Jesus were completely turned round. They met him: He was alive again.

Filled with faith and courage, they went out for Jesus into the whole known world. They were fearless people. They knew that Jesus had conquered death. So whatever happened, they knew they were safe in God's hands.

It's very different today. We live two thousand years later. Not many of us are fearless. Many, instead, are understandably afraid of dying.

But Paul tells us to be as confident as those first followers. Jesus really has conquered death. And if the Spirit is living inside us we will follow in his footsteps.

Read Romans 8:11

> If the Spirit of God, who raised Jesus from death, lives in you, then he who raised Christ from death will also give life to your mortal bodies by the presence of his Spirit in you.

Someone once said, 'I'd rather live a short life about something, than a long life about nothing.' That's a good motto for a Christian. Full of faith in God we're to live whole-heartedly for him. For we know that not even death can really harm us. Death simply takes us home to be with God.

23

Shade in the bar to the extent that you believe Jesus rose from the dead

Don't believe **Believe**

Now tick the sentence that best puts into words how you feel.

☐ I am afraid of dying and cannot bear to think about it.
☐ I never really think about my own death.
☐ I don't mind the thought of dying because when you die you die.
☐ I look forward to dying because I'm going to a better place.
☐ I'm afraid of dying and want to believe in life after death.
☐ Other ....
....
....
....

YIPEE!! DEATH IS DEAD!!!

Lord Jesus, you know I'm sometimes afraid of death. So pour your Spirit into me, the Spirit that raised you from the dead. And may I follow in your footsteps. Amen.

24

Born of the Spirit

We come now to the third section of the book. We've traced the story of the Spirit (units 1–8). We've looked at the Bible's pictures of the Spirit (units 9–23). Now our task is to see how all of this applies to us today.

I've met loads of young Christians eaten up with worry: 'Do I have the Spirit? Don't I have the Spirit? How will I know if I have him or not?'

Here's a simple exercise that will either set your mind at rest, or challenge you to take further action.

24

Tick each box if the statement applies to you.

☐ I believe in God
☐ I want to follow Jesus

If you've put two ticks, the Holy Spirit is at work in your life. You can't even get as far as you've got without him.

Read John 3:5–6

> 'I am telling you the truth,' replied Jesus. 'No one can enter the Kingdom of God without being born of water and the Spirit. A person is born physically of human parents, but is born spiritually of the Spirit.'

Some people say you become a Christian first, then at a later stage receive God's Holy Spirit. Jesus tells you otherwise. You can't even begin your Christian journey without the Spirit.

So if you ticked both boxes, the Spirit is working in you. But it's likely you're at the very beginning of the journey. God has so much in store for you! Just begin safe in the knowledge that God's Spirit is with you. Then look for ways in which his Spirit will work more powerfully in you.

Holy Spirit, you brought me to new birth. You will be with me as I grow. When the time is right, show me more and more of yourself. Amen.

P.S. If you couldn't tick both boxes, grab your youth leader or minister and talk it over.

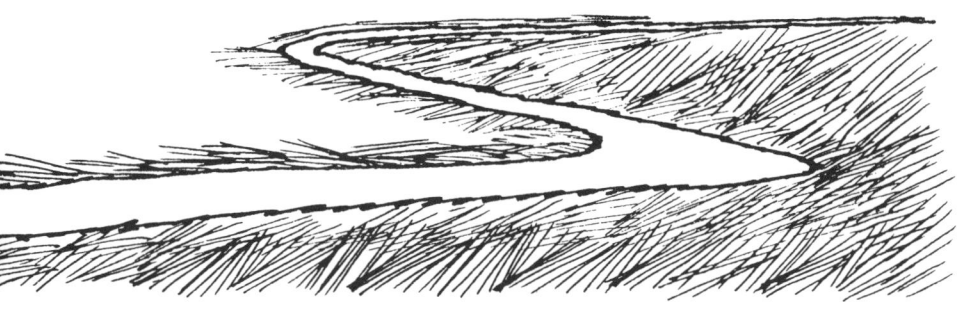

25 The father's joy

Here are some words to describe fathers. Tick the ones which apply to God the Father.

☐ Stern
☐ Kind
☐ Generous
☐ Bald
☐ Bad-tempered
☐ Patient
☐ Unfit
☐ Fair

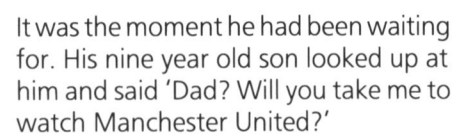

It was the moment he had been waiting for. His nine year old son looked up at him and said 'Dad? Will you take me to watch Manchester United?'

He couldn't have asked for anything better. His Dad had supported United all his life. All his life he'd looked forward to taking his child to the ground.

Imagine his son's excitement on going to the ground for the first time. Imagine how pleased his Dad is to give his child what he'd always wanted to give him.

If you can imagine that, you'll understand a bit more about God. He longs to hear us say 'please fill us with your Holy Spirit'. When we say it he is overjoyed. It gives him just as much pleasure to give us his Spirit as it gives us to receive him.

25

Read Luke 11:11–13

Would any of you who are fathers give your son a snake when he asks for a fish? Or would you give him a scorpion when he asks for an egg? Bad as you are, you know how to give good things to your children. How much more, then, will the Father in heaven give the Holy Spirit to those who ask him!

Lord God, thank you that you're my perfect father. When we ask for your Holy Spirit you're delighted to answer us. So I come to you now. Please fill me with your Spirit. Amen.

An important step in letting God's Holy Spirit work in us is to know what God is really like. He's not some stingy tight-fisted kill-joy. He loves to give you good gifts.

So if you're ready, ask him to fill you with the Holy Spirit. Then believe he's answered your prayer. And look out for ways in which his Spirit is at work in you.

I THOUGHT YOU'D NEVER ASK!!

26
Drenched with God

26

The service had just finished. People were milling around. All of a sudden I felt prompted by God to ask for his Spirit to work more powerfully in me.

I told a friend, and together we knelt down. He prayed for me. He asked God's Holy Spirit to take me a stage further in my Christian journey.

Even then I wasn't prepared for what happened. A torrent of worship came welling up inside me. I'd never felt so close to God. I went to one side of the church, where I knelt and simply couldn't stop the flow of praise.

Here's how John the Baptist describes what happened to me that night. He's speaking about Jesus.

Read Matthew 3:11

> I baptise you with water to show that you have repented, but the one who will come after me will baptise you with the Holy Spirit and fire. He is much greater than I am; and I am not good enough even to carry his sandals.

According to John, Jesus was to baptize with the Holy Spirit. And to 'baptize' something means to drench it through and through: to give it a really good soaking.

That's what happened to me after that service. Jesus 'drenched' me with God. His Spirit soaked me in God's presence. I was *'baptized with the Holy Spirit'*.

That doesn't mean I didn't have the Spirit before. It's just that God wanted to take me further. It doesn't mean he'll do it for you in the same way: we're all different. But remain open to God. And when the time is right his Spirit will drench you with the presence of God.

Put a cross on the line where you think you are now.

_____

I want nothing to do with the Holy Spirit　　　　**I'd like to be 'drenched with the Spirit'**

Lord Jesus, thank you that your Spirit is with me. I don't want to run before I can walk, but I do want to go further. When the time is right, Lord Jesus, please drench me with your Spirit. Amen.

27 Receive

It was Carla's birthday. Early in the morning, before anybody was about, a friend crept up to her front door. By it she left a parcel, beautifully wrapped. Then she crept away again.

Carla got up, got ready, and set off for school. But she totally ignored the parcel. She ignored it later when she got back. Weeks later it's still there, the paper wet and soggy from the rain.

A present is no use if it's not opened. So God can offer the gift of his Holy Spirit till he's blue in the face. But until we receive it, it won't be ours.

The thing is . . . how do I receive it?

Let Peter tell you how.

> Each one of you must turn away from his sins and be baptised in the name of Jesus Christ, so that your sins will be forgiven; and you will receive God's gift, the Holy Spirit.
>
> Acts 2:38

The most important of those words is '*turn*'. If you want to receive God's Holy Spirit, turn. Turn round and open yourself to God. Ask him to fill you with his Spirit. He will be true to his promise.

Take a glass and hold it upside down under a running tap. There's water round it, but none gets in. That's just like the person who wants nothing to do with God. The Holy Spirit can't get a look in.

Now turn the glass round. What happens? Write it in this space:

....

....

the gift
27

Holy Spirit, like that glass I turn round. I turn round to you. Fill me to overflowing with your Spirit. Then let your life flow out from me. Amen.

28

Robert was fed up with London. All that concrete. He wanted space! He wanted to breath! He wanted the Highlands of Scotland.

So he jumped on his Suzuki, filled up at Hammersmith, and set off. He passed Birmingham. He passed Manchester. He passed Carlisle... all without stopping.

He passed Glasgow, and the wilds began to open up before him. He began to relax and breathe. But in the first really wild space he got to his bike spluttered to a halt. The petrol tank was empty. He was miles from the nearest garage.

If you keep running on one tank of petrol, you'll run out sooner or later. You need to keep stopping off to refuel.

It's just the same for the Christian. You can't run for ever on one spiritual high. Try it and you'll soon hit the ground with a bump. You need to keep coming back for more fuel.

Read Ephesians 5:18

Do not get drunk with wine, which will only ruin you; instead, be filled with the Spirit.

Keep refuelling

SPLUTTER! SLUTTER!!

28

The words *'be filled with the Spirit'* really mean *'Go on being filled with the Spirit'*. So make time, day by day, to open yourself to God. Ask him to fill you with his Spirit every day. Then, unlike Robert, you'll be able to keep going. You'll be able to journey on. You'll grow stronger in the Christian life, and get to know God better and better.

Father God, you give us the power to follow Jesus. Help me to go on being filled with your Spirit, make me strong for the journey, and help me to know you more and more. Amen.

Draw a line to link each object with the correct fuel.

InterCity 125	Aviation fuel
Concorde	Liquid Nitrogen
A Christian	A nuclear core
Space Shuttle	Diesel oil
Milk float	The Holy Spirit
Popeye	Electric battery
Long-distance submarine	Spinach

29

Simon's parents were devastated. They really had tried to give him everything. Without smothering him, they'd always gone out of their way to make sure he was OK.

Now he stood in the dock accused of burglary. And as the 'guilty' verdict rang out, his parents wept. They couldn't believe he would hurt other people like this. They loved him so much.

That's why it hurt. It hurt so much because they loved him so much. Love's like that. It makes you care about people and about what they do.

But a parent's love for their child is only a faint echo of the love of God. Imagine how he feels when his people let him down.

Read Ephesians 4:30

> *And do no not make God's Holy Spirit sad; for the Spirit is God's mark of ownership on you, a guarantee that the Day will come when God will set you free.*

God loves us perfectly. He sends his Holy Spirit into the life of anyone open to him. So let's not make the Holy Spirit sad. Let's not hurt him by the things we do and say. Let's go out of our way to please the Spirit within us.

Which of these things would most hurt the Holy Spirit? Tick it, and then write the opposite to it in the box provided.

☐ Ignoring the cries of the starving

☐ Refusing to go further in the Christian faith

☐ Being really into God and then forgetting him

☐ Abusing people of another race

☐ Pretending to be something you're not

29

Hurting love

Holy Spirit, thank you that you live inside me. I don't want to make you sad. So help me to please you with my words, with my thoughts, with my actions. Amen.

30

On a trip to Jerusalem, Jesus and his disciples visited the temple. The disciples were impressed. *'Look, Teacher!'* they said, *'what wonderful stones and buildings'*.

Jesus was less impressed. He knew that huge buildings for worship meant nothing unless they were filled with real worship. *'Anyway'*, Jesus told them, *'you see these great buildings? Everyone of them will be thrown down'*.

Jesus was right. The great temple at Jerusalem was destroyed. But that doesn't mean God no longer has a temple. He does still have a temple, and it's nearer to you than you think. Go and look in a mirror. As you look at your reflection, read these words.

Read 1 Corinthians 6:19

> *Don't you know that your body is the temple of the Holy Spirit, who lives in you and who was given to you by God? You do not belong to yourselves but to God.*

Porta-te

30

The temple of stone was destroyed. But today you are God's temple. God lives in you by his Holy Spirit. You're a porta-temple! Wherever you go, God goes with you.

Here's a list of things that would have happened in the temple. How many of them happen inside you? Tick them.

Thank you Holy Spirit, you live inside me. May my life be a true temple full of real worship. Amen.

☐ Worship of God
☐ Prayer for the needs of other people
☐ Forgiving other people
☐ Hearing and acting on God's message
☐ Giving to the poor

mples

31

Listen! We have good news! Jesus of Nazareth has conquered death! He was killed, by being nailed to a cross. We buried him. But now we've met him again. He's alive! No-one need ever fear death again!

With a message like that, you'd imagine that Jesus' first followers would have found plenty of people to listen. Indeed they did, and the church grew quickly.

But not everyone wanted to listen. Some very powerful people were enraged by the disciples' message about Jesus. So they threw Paul and the others out of cities, flogged and stoned them.

But when the going got tough, Jesus' followers could always call on the Spirit's help. Jesus had promised his power for anyone who wanted to tell others about him.

Read Acts 1:8

But when the Holy Spirit comes upon you, you will be filled with power, and you will be witnesses for me in Jerusalem, in all Judaea and Samaria, and to the ends of the earth.

My witnesses

31

Just like those early disciples, we are called to tell others about Jesus. For we are *'witnesses'* of all good things that God has done.

But just like those early disciples, we often meet people who don't want to hear. At times like that things can get tough, and we can be tempted to pack in.

But the Holy Spirit's power is there just for moments like that. If you want to tell other people about Jesus, his promise is that the Spirit will give you the power to do it.

If you were to tell somebody about Jesus, what kind of thing would you want to say? Write it in this space.

....

....

....

Now think about who you can tell. Someone who doesn't know Jesus yet. Write their name in this space.

....

Lord Jesus, I am your witness. By your Spirit, give me courage: help me to speak clearly and honestly for you. Amen.

32

What next?

The *Following Jesus* Series

If you have enjoyed using *The Spirit of Jesus*, you might like to look at other titles in the series. All are available singly or in packs of 10 copies.

Following Jesus presents a lively and stimulating introduction to the Christian faith in words and cartoons. Suitable for use as a confirmation course, the 31 steps/units (with practical suggestions and prayers) cover the basics of Christian teaching and discipleship. An additional leaflet is available which provides leaders with suggestions for four weekly sessions.

The Power of Jesus contains 28 units which consider the power of Jesus as seen in the seven signs in John's Gospel.

Picturing Jesus contains 28 units which consider the seven 'I Am' sayings in John's Gospel—the pictures which Jesus used to illustrate and show who he was: 'I am the Good Shepherd', 'I am the Vine', 'I am the Bread of Life', 'I am the Way, the Truth and the Life', 'I am the Light of the World', 'I am the Resurrection and the Life', 'I am the Gate'.

Stories by Jesus contains 31 units which consider ways Jesus used parables to illustrate his teaching and shows how they still relate to and challenge us 2000 years later.

Surprised by Jesus contains 31 units which consider ways in which Jesus surprised people by what he said and what he did.

Another 7 titles are planned in the *Following Jesus* series, including new editions of *Serving Jesus* and *Praying with Jesus*.

All titles in the series are illustrated throughout by Taffy.

Following Jesus, *The Power of Jesus*, *Picturing Jesus*, *Stories by Jesus* and *Surprised by Jesus* are available now from all good Christian bookshops, or in case of difficulty from BRF, Peter's Way, Sandy Lane West, Oxford, OX4 5HG.

If you would like to know more about the full range of Bible reading notes and other Bible reading group study materials published by BRF, write and ask for a free catalogue.